Southern Utah ... parks than any ... one has its ow ... these places, Zion National Park is the crown jewel.

With towering sandstone cliffs, deeply entrenched canyons, curvaceous hidden coves, and lush hanging gardens, Zion gives the explorer an impressive array of stellar adventures. This book will help you make the most of your time there and help you experience more of what it has to offer.

There are a number of things to take into account before exploring Zion National Park:

FLASH FLOODS - The narrow canyons of Zion can present real dangers during or after a storm. in some canyons it is not even possible to climb to safety. Always know the weather and conditions before entering any narrow canyon. This information can be found at the visitor center.

HIGH CLIFFS - There are a number of trails in Zion that have very exposed drop-offs. People have fallen to their deaths. Pay close attention to your children and avoid these hikes if you have a fear of heights.

WILDLIFE - The park is a great place to spot all sorts of animals in their natural environment. From desert big-horn sheep to canyon tree frogs there are wild animals of all shapes and sizes. The important thing to remember is that they are exactly that - wild animals. Do not feed, approach, or harass the wildlife. Enjoy them from afar and take as many pictures as you like.

PERSONAL SAFETY - Some of Zion's best adventures don't follow trails at all. Hikers may end up wading or swimming through deep pools of water, climbing over obstacles of varying difficulty, or utilizing route finding skills. Be sure to know your abilities and stay within them. Your safety is your responsibility.

GO PREPARED - If you're going into the wilderness, be sure you are equipped to come back as well. Staying hydrated, knowing your limits, and taking the right gear will help ensure many future adventures.

LEAVE NO TRACE - Having a minimal impact on nature is what we should all strive for. If you take something in, be sure to bring it out as well. The best way for future generations to enjoy these natural treasures is to leave them as undisturbed as possible (www.lnt.org).

PARK CONTACT INFORMATION:
Phone: 435-772-3256
Website: www.nps.gov/zion

MAIN MAP

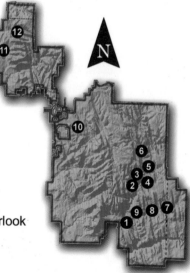

1. Watchman Trail
2. Emerald Pools
3. Angels Landing
4. Hidden Canyon
5. Observation Point
6. The Narrows
7. Clear Creek
8. Canyon Overlook
9. Lower Pine Creek
10. Kolob Terrace
11. Taylor Creek
12. Timber Creek Overlook

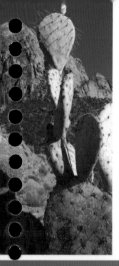

The Watchman Trail takes you beside the Virgin River before heading upwards to a lookout with nice views of the lower part of Zion Canyon. It passes a small spring and plenty of cacti, pinyons, and junipers. Although much of the trail has exposure to drop-offs, they are rather tame by Zion standards. It is best done in the morning or evening to avoid the heat.

AT A GLANCE

- Round trip distance is 2.6 miles
- Elevation change is 368 feet
- Allow 2 to 3 hours
- Flat initially, then steady incline
- Well worn path is easy to follow
- Minor exposure to drop-offs
- Toilets at the visitor center

Difficulty ranking in book

easiest ⬤ hardest

LOCATION

From Springdale take Hwy 9 into the park. Once through the entrance gate, take an immediate right into the visitor center. The trailhead is on the east side of the bridge crossing the Virgin River.

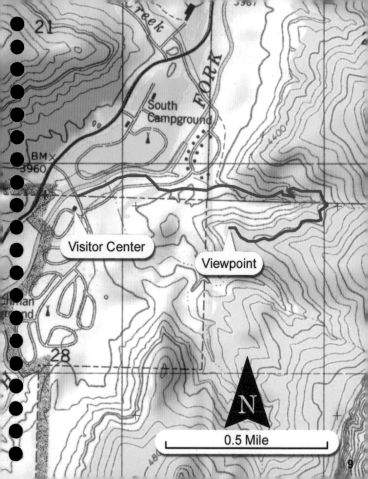

21

Creek D FORK

3967

South
Campground

4400

BM ×
3960

Visitor Center

Viewpoint

man
und

28

N

0.5 Mile

9

Zion's Emerald Pools are a popular destination because of their easy access and great scenery. With its ribbons of waterfalls, the Lower Pool is the easiest to reach along a half mile

paved path. Reaching the Upper and Middle Pools requires a more strenuous (albeit short) route that includes navigating a rock staircase wedged between some gigantic boulders.

11

AT A GLANCE

- Distances (round trip): Lower Pool 1.2 miles, Middle Pool 1.6 miles, Upper Pool 2.2 miles
- Elevation change: Lower Pool 69 feet, Middle Pool 150 feet, Upper Pool 350 feet
- Allow 1 to 2 hours
- Gradual incline to Lower Pool, then steep grade to Middle and Upper Pools
- Paved to Lower Pool, then more rugged and uneven surface to Middle and Upper Pools
- Well marked and easy to follow trail
- Exposed drop-offs
- Toilets at Zion Lodge shuttle stop

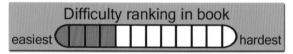

Difficulty ranking in book

easiest | hardest

LOCATION

From Springdale take Hwy 9 into the park and take the first right into the visitor center. Take the free shuttle provided by the park to Zion Lodge. Cross the road to find the trailhead.

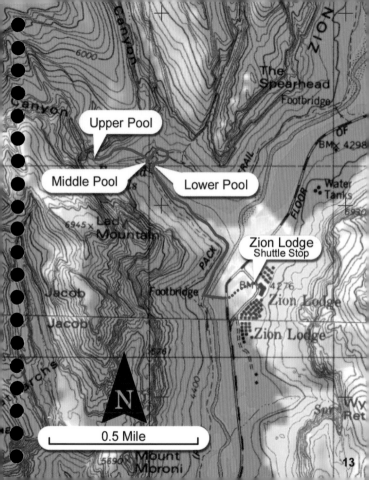

Upper Pool

Middle Pool

Lower Pool

Zion Lodge
Shuttle Stop

N

0.5 Mile

13

This adventure is the perfect way to test your fear of heights. The Angels Landing Trail is an engineering marvel that utilizes switchbacks to work its way up a cliff face. It cuts through a shady canyon, and takes you across a narrow ridge of rock with chain railings to deliver you to the awe-inspiring summit. No wonder this is considered a Zion classic.

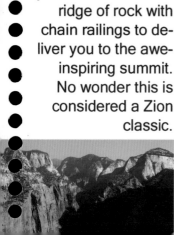

AT A GLANCE

- Distances (round trip): Scout Lookout 4 miles, Angels Landing 5.4 miles
- Elevation change: Scout Lookout 955 feet, Angels Landing 1488 feet
- Allow 3 to 5 hours
- Consistently steep
- Mostly paved trail until Scout Lookout, then rock scrambling to Angels Landing
- Well marked and easy to follow trail
- VERY exposed to long drop-offs
- Toilets at shuttle bus stop

Difficulty ranking in book

easiest ⟨ ⟩ hardest

LOCATION

From Springdale take Hwy 9 into the park. Once through the entrance gate, take an immediate right into the visitor center. Take the free shuttle provided by the park to The Grotto. Cross the road to the trailhead.

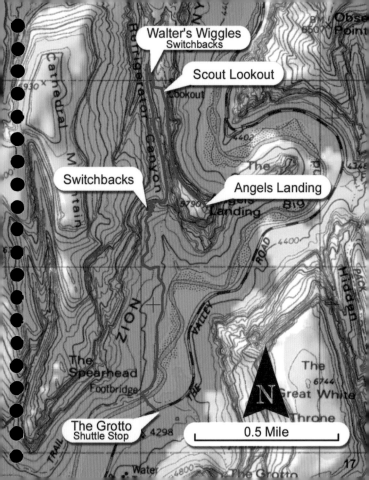

4 Hidden Canyon

The Hidden Canyon Trail offers a peek into one of Zion's many hanging canyons. A precarious route takes you across a chiseled out section of an exposed cliff with a chain handrail for your safety. It's an exhilarating experience that takes you to the mouth of Hidden Canyon that offers plenty of additional exploring if you so desire.

AT A GLANCE

- Round trip distance is 2.4 miles but more exploration is possible up canyon past the trail
- Elevation change is 850 feet
- Allow 1 to 3 hours
- Consistently steep
- Roughly paved trail surface that changes to rock and sand for last half mile.
- Well marked and easy to follow trail
- VERY exposed to long drop-offs
- Pit toilets at the trailhead

Difficulty ranking in book

easiest ⬤⬤⬤⬤⬤⬤⬤⬤☐☐ hardest

LOCATION

From Springdale take Hwy 9 into the park. Once through the entrance gate, take an immediate right into the visitor center. Take the free shuttle provided by the park to Weeping Rock. The trailhead is at the edge of the parking lot.

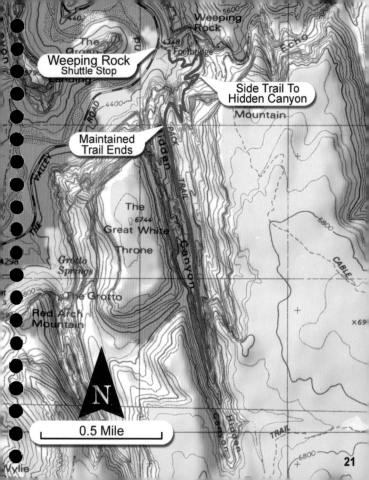

Weeping Rock
Shuttle Stop

Side Trail To
Hidden Canyon

Maintained
Trail Ends

N

0.5 Mile

21

Observation Point offers some of the best views in all of Zion Canyon. It actually looks down on Angels Landing! The trail passes through a section of Echo Canyon where you can view into the depths of a truly serpentine slot canyon. This route climbs over 2000 vertical feet and is worth every step.

AT A GLANCE

- Round trip distance is 8 miles
- Elevation change is 2148 feet
- Allow 4 to 7 hours
- Mostly steep grade with some level sections
- Most of the trail length has a rough, unevenly paved surface
- Well marked and easy to follow
- Exposed drop-offs
- Pit toilets at the trailhead

Difficulty ranking in book

easiest | | | | | | | | | | | hardest

LOCATION

From Springdale take Hwy 9 into the park. Once through the entrance gate, take an immediate right into the visitor center. Take the free shuttle provided by the park to Weeping Rock. The trailhead is at the edge of the parking lot.

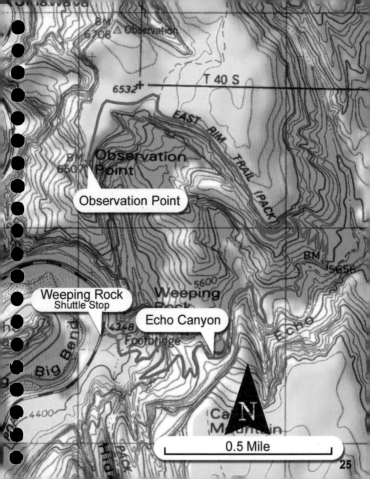

Zion Narrows are one of the best adventures in the entire South-west. The Virgin River cuts this amazing canyon through vertical sandstone walls over 1000 feet high in places. The result is a breathtaking journey filled with rock, water, and hanging gardens. Whether you want to stick to the one mile paved path or venture on and get wet, the Narrows offers something for everyone.

AT A GLANCE

- Round trip distances: end of pavement 2.2 miles, Orderville Canyon 5 miles, Big Spring 9.4 miles
- Elevation change to Big Spring is 334 feet
- Allow 1 to 8 hours depending on destination
- Paved trail for first 1.1 miles, then the route becomes the river itself
- Tricky footing along with wading/swimming
- Check conditions at visitor center for safety
- Toilets at the trailhead - carry out all waste beyond this point

Difficulty ranking in book

easiest [||||||||||||] hardest

LOCATION

From Springdale take Hwy 9 into the park. Once through the entrance gate, take an immediate right into the visitor center. Take the free shuttle provided by the park to Temple of Sinawava. The adventure starts here.

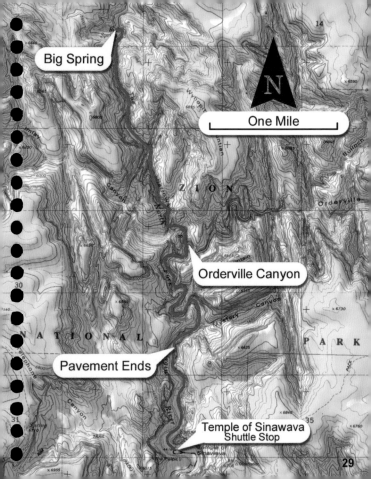

Big Spring

N

One Mile

Orderville Canyon

Pavement Ends

Temple of Sinawava
Shuttle Stop

29

One of the best ways to explore the east side of Zion National Park is via the Clear Creek drainage. Clear Creek (usually dry) runs alongside the road on the east side of the park and is surrounded by a designated wilderness area. Its easy access allows you to explore as much or as little as you like. You can expect great views, a number of narrow passages, and very few people.

AT A GLANCE

- Distance and elevation change can be as little or as much as you wish
- Flash flood potential so be sure to check the weather and conditions before entering
- Allow at least 1 hour, but many can be spent here
- No actual trail, just follows the creekbed
- Good route finding skills recommended
- No toilets at pullouts

Difficulty ranking in book

easiest ⬚⬚⬚⬚⬚⬚⬚⬚⬚⬚ hardest

LOCATION

Enter the park from the east side on Hwy 9. Soon after the entry gate, pass Checkerboard Mesa. The creek drainage (usually dry) that runs next to the road is where this adventure takes place. Several pullouts from Checkerboard Mesa to the Zion-Mt. Carmel Tunnel allow access to the drainage.

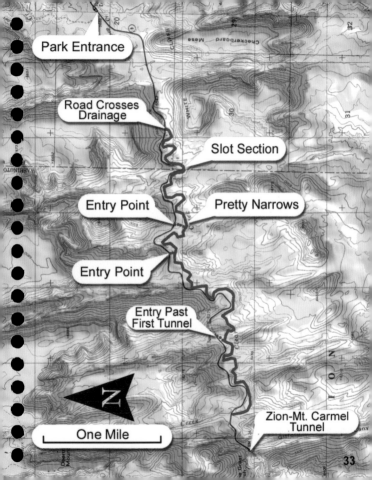

Park Entrance

Road Crosses Drainage

Slot Section

Entry Point

Pretty Narrows

Entry Point

Entry Past First Tunnel

Zion-Mt. Carmel Tunnel

N

One Mile

33

This short path curves along the cliffs above Pine Creek slot canyon on its way to an overlook atop a sheer cliff. Handrails help keep things safe both at the lookout and on the trail. Enjoy looking into the dark abyss of the slot canyon below as you make your way to the jaw dropping finale with some of the best views on the east side of the park.

AT A GLANCE

- Round trip distance is 1 mile
- Elevation change is 163 feet
- Allow 1 hour
- Steep initially, then levels out
- Well maintained trail, but surfaces are uneven and footing can be tricky
- Exposure to long drop-offs, but railings keep most areas safe
- Pit toilets at parking lot

Difficulty ranking in book

easiest |▌▌▌▌▌| hardest

LOCATION

From Springdale take Hwy 9 into the park. Once through the entrance gate, continue on Hwy 9 through the Zion-Mt. Carmel Tunnel. Parking is immediately after the tunnel on the right. Overflow parking is a bit further on the left. The trailhead is directly across the road from the parking lot.

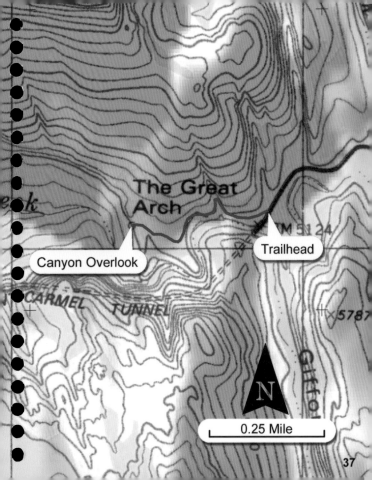

The Great Arch

Canyon Overlook

M 5124

Trailhead

CARMEL TUNNEL

5787

Giffo

N

0.25 Mile

37

Lower Pine Creek is a great place to spend some time climbing from boulder to boulder, soaking your feet in crystal clear pools of water, or even hanging out at the base of a peaceful waterfall. This can be a strenuous obstacle course, but the access is easy, the scenery amazing, and the crowds are generally somewhere else.

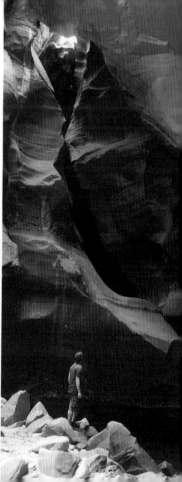

AT A GLANCE

- Distances (round trip): lower waterfall 0.6 miles, upper chamber 1.6 miles
- Elevation change: lower waterfall 50 feet, upper chamber 340 feet
- Allow 1 to 4 hours depending on destination
- Route is really an obstacle course and not a trail at all
- Lots of boulder hopping, rock scrambling, and route finding
- No toilets available

Difficulty ranking in book

easiest ▢▢▢▢▢▢□□□□□ hardest

LOCATION

From Springdale take Hwy 9 into the park. Once through the entrance gate, continue on Hwy 9 toward the Zion-Mt. Carmel Tunnel. At both the first and third switchbacks are pullouts that allow access to Lower Pine Creek.

40

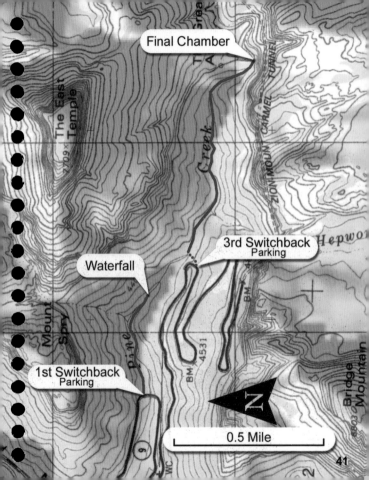

Final Chamber

3rd Switchback
Parking

Waterfall

1st Switchback
Parking

N

0.5 Mile

41

Kolob Terrace is a lesser known section of the park that provides plenty of potential for exploring or just taking a leisurely drive through some very scenic terrain that is surrounded by designated wilderness area. From the top of the park views at Lava Point to the rugged adventure of Grapevine Spring, Kolob Terrace offers a break from the crowds in a truly pristine environment.

AT A GLANCE

- Distance from Virgin to Lava Point Lookout is 21.7 miles
- Elevation at Lava Point is 7890 feet
- Allow 1 to 2 hours to drive the road, more for exploring
- Several trailheads that provide access to both primitive trails and some more maintained
- Pit toilets are located at Left Fork, Hop Valley, Wildcat Canyon, and Lava Point Campground
- The road to Lava Point is closed in Winter.

Difficulty ranking in book

easiest ▢▢▢▢▢▢▢▢▢▢ hardest

Difficulty ranking based on the walk to Lava Point but harder options are available

LOCATION

From Springdale take Hwy 9 west for about 12 miles to the town of Virgin. In Virgin turn right on Kolob Reservoir Road. After about 7 miles begins the Kolob Terrace section of Zion.

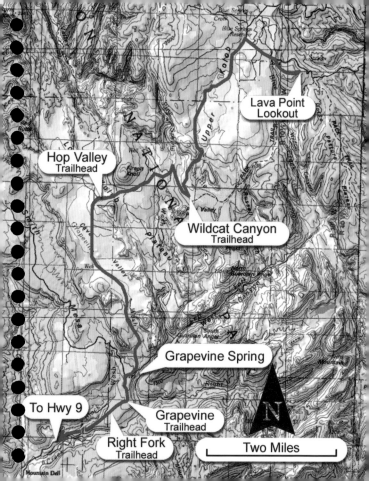

Lava Point
Lookout

Hop Valley
Trailhead

Wildcat Canyon
Trailhead

Grapevine Spring

To Hwy 9

Grapevine
Trailhead

Right Fork
Trailhead

N

Two Miles

The trail to the Middle Fork of Taylor Creek is a great way to experience the Kolob Canyons section of the park. Stroll along a gentle stream and past a pair of old homesteads as the surrounding red rock cliffs stretch to the sky. The path ends at the enormous Double Arch Alcove, putting a final exclamation point on a great hike.

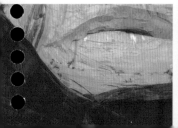

AT A GLANCE

- Round trip distance is 5 miles
- Elevation change is 450 feet
- Allow 3 to 5 hours
- Steep descent in the beginning, then gradual steady incline
- Well worn path with many creek crossings
- Easy to follow trail
- This hike is in a designated wilderness area
- Toilets at visitor center NOT at the trailhead

Difficulty ranking in book

easiest |■■■■■■■|□□□□| hardest

LOCATION

Take exit 40 on Interstate 15 to the Kolob Canyons section of Zion National Park. Pay the entrance fee at the visitor center and continue 2 miles up the road to the Taylor Creek Trailhead on the left.

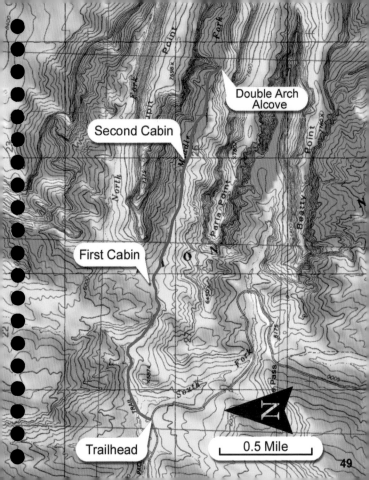

Double Arch Alcove

Second Cabin

First Cabin

Trailhead

0.5 Mile

49

The best thing about the Timber Creek Overlook may be the drive to the trailhead. The
views of the Kolob Canyons from the road are
stunning. The short trail from the parking area
is worth the extra effort as it takes you to a
viewpoint with an expansive panorama of the
Timber Creek drainage and beyond.

AT A GLANCE

- Round trip distance is 1 mile
- Elevation change is 100 feet
- Allow 1 hour
- Easy grade, not much up and down
- Well maintained trail and easy to follow
- Pit toilets at trailhead

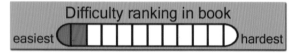

Difficulty ranking in book

easiest ◀ hardest ▶

LOCATION

Take exit 40 on Interstate 15 to the Kolob Canyons section of Zion National Park. Pay the entrance fee at the visitor center and continue 5 miles up the road to where it ends at the Kolob Canyons Viewpoint. The trailhead is located here.

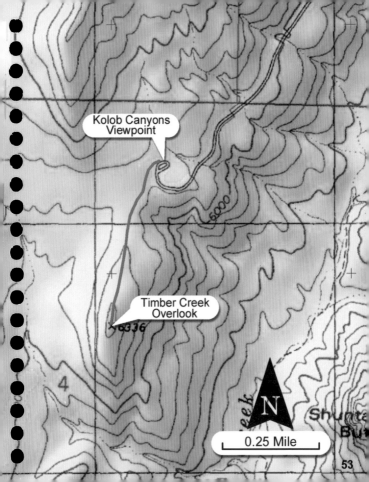

Kolob Canyons
Viewpoint

Timber Creek
Overlook

5000

×6336

N

Shunta
Bu

0.25 Mile

53

NOTES

Pocket
Adventure
Guide™

Exploring Zion

By Dave Marriner
maps provided by mytopo.com

TABLE OF CONTENTS